# Deceit

## Barbara Louiz

Copyright © 2024 by Barbara Louiz

All rights reserved.

No portion of this book may be reproduced in any form without written permission from the publisher or author, except as permitted by U.S. copyright law.

# Contents

1. Epilogue: Misha     1
2. Epilogue: Joe     15
3. Epilogue: Ross     25
4. Epilogue: Hans     38

# Epilogue: Misha

**1** Month Later

"Joe," I sighed.

"Mm, yeah, say it just like that."

"Joe." This time, I followed it up with a little shove. The alpha still stayed glued, stubbornly, to my neck. I could feel his smile against my skin. When he didn't let up, I felt an elbow to the ribs was in order.

"Oof-! Gah-! What the hell?"

"We're going to be late," I said.

"Late for what? Central Park stays open till 1 am!"

"Ah, yes, because we'll want to stay in a big, dark, empty park till 1 in the morning."

"You could take down three full grown male alphas if you wanted to!" Joe argued. I would have taken it as a compliment if not for the fact that he was trying to keep me caged between him and the kitchen counter. Some silly thinking of mine had me assured Joe would be less of a nuisance with Hans, Ross, and even Conrad around. Oh, how naive I was. By some remarkable ingenuity, the alpha still had time to catch me in his hormone-driven state.

I heaved out a sigh and slipped past him, the black trench coat catching my eye in the distant corner of the kitchen. "Conrad's been waiting in the car for ten minutes and with you it'll turn into an hour."

Joe followed me as I slipped on the coat and searched for my keys on the hooks above the dining table. He crossed his arms and smiled. "Is that really a bad thing, though? We'll ask him to join us."

I snorted. "He's barely shown interest in kissing or cuddling. I highly doubt he'd be down for a spur of the moment threesome."

There was an unbidden silence that followed as I located the keys and went for the closet by the front doors. Joe followed but didn't comment. Something shifted in the air. A complete one-eighty. Those seemed to be more common around here now.

When I finally managed to wrangle my old boots on, Joe spoke up.

"If shit hits the fan today, don't take it too hard. Con would have left by now if he didn't think we were worth it."

I smiled wryly as I looked up at him. Joe was a strange package of contradictions and mild chaos. He liked to keep the pain and emotions deep down like the good alpha son of old money and purported nobility. Ironically, he was the most emotionally volatile of us next to Conrad. His feelings and sentiments came out in a rushing explosion of rage, panic, or frustration like the eruption of a supervolcano. It was an easy doorway for a look into the state of his thoughts. Right now, the peak inside made it very clear that Joe was hurting and would hurt if Conrad ever decided to leave. The idea that the red-headed delta was hanging on for this long for a reason was particularly appealing to someone who couldn't face the truth.

The truth being that we'd messed up and Conrad owed us nothing. The truth that he could be hanging on out of spite, boredom, or apathy. Maybe even pity. The truth being that I might even deserve the pain.

I mulled this over as I smiled up at the alpha with the nervous tick in his eye that he tried hard to cover up. Unlike Joe, I knew how to keep the mask on. Even when it hurt the most.

"I'm fine. I'll be fine. Conrad and I are just having a simple talk."

He looked a little skeptical. Was my mask slipping? Was I getting old at the game? I shook my head, gave him a hesitant kiss and stepped out into the gentle light of the warmer-than-usual winter afternoon. My heart swelled a little, catching sight of Conrad in the passenger seat of the Rolls Royce, distracted by something on his phone.

"Hey," I said once I reached the car. He glanced up for a second. His eyes jumped down to his phone just as quickly.

"Hey," he muttered.

Right. That's how it was going to be. That's how it had been for a while.

I pulled out of the driveway. It was the perfect winter day for a stroll through Central Park. The snow was light and mostly melted and the air carried a warmth closer to spring. The sun was just as bright. The only thing to hamper the mood was the current situation.

"How was your day?"

"Fine."

A pause. I tried again. "Did you enjoy breakfast? Heard you and Hans went to a cafe."

"Yeah."

Joe would have growled and demanded that the delta stop being so obtuse. Ross might have laughed and asked a question that would require more than a one word answer. Hans was the only one to open him up. As it was, I had little to no real social grace or understanding unless it was under the mask of a persona going undercover. I grew up taught to never be myself. How I could make Conrad understand and trust us again with who I truly was left me at a loss. What I was was a mess. A toy soldier taking orders from his betters. A good beta under the control of alphas and stronger betas most his life.

I mulled over these thoughts. Something about this drive to Central Park felt more final than heading into a shootout. I had never wanted anything in my meager life. Conrad, I wanted. And I had probably fucked up the one chance I'd been given. This felt more like the last nail in the coffin to something that could have let me into a little bit of happiness had I not been the pathetic and incompetent man that I was.

"We're here."

I jumped a little at the words, realizing, with some giddy excitement, that Conrad had spoken of his own volition. We parked and headed out. I realized, with some growing dread and anxiety, that Conrad seemed none to happy when he realized the path I was taking him down. He seemed even more perturbed at the sight of the bench facing the angles we had seen the first time.

"Erm, do-do you want to sit down?" I smiled and sat, patting the spot next to me. At first, it seemed like the bit of hesitance guarding him would dissipate. I was crushed when he shrugged and stayed standing. I could feel my throat clog.

There was a small silence not completely uncomfortable. Crows cawed by the statues and the snow surrounding the area seemed to bring about a peace and beauty. Still, I struggled to push away the urge to shut-down and put on a mask of passivity and indifference.

The delta stuffed his hands in his coat pockets. I noted that his red hair looked striking among the whiteness of the park.

"So, what's up? You said you wanted to talk?"

I tried reading him, Conrad always having been an open book. Today wasn't exactly bringing out my A-game and I only had a vague sense of discomfort and apathy. I slumped. Suppose it was time to come out with it. I could always crawl into a closet and wait for the pain to go away if nothing good came of it. It was something I was used to doing.

I wrangled my hands and sighed. "Let's come out with it. I cheated on you with Ross. I had sex with him in the apartment we shared. I convinced myself it didn't matter because you were a cover story to get to Seraz. And I...." I choked up. Which was ridiculous. Only Conrad had the right.

It had been a long time but I felt words cut their way into my head and scream into my ears. Pathetic. Useless. Degenerate piece of--

"Woah, woah, Misha? Misha!"

I sucked in a breath as I heard Conrad's voice through the haze. A glance up and I looked into startled wide eyes and paler-than-usual skin. There was confusion and maybe even a move to comfort me. Still, his hesitance took over and he stood back with a look of apprehension.

"You-you ok?"

"Yeah," I said. My voice came out as an unsteady whisper. I took another breath. "Sorry. I-god, I'm sorry."

"What was that? You were looking behind me like there was kind of god-damned serial killer with an axe raised." I didn't blame his startled state. My face must have looked a chalky white.

"I'm sorry," was all that came out. "If you want to leave..."

I honestly thought he would take that as a great opportunity to bust on a pathetic beta who'd done nothing but hurt him. I would understand even if it hurt. Instead, he stayed. Moreover, he sat down.

Warily and at a distance unsurprisingly but something lifted in me for a moment. I glanced over at him while he paused to look down at his gloved hands.

"What was that?"

I blinked and tried to focus on the question. I swallowed a lump. "It just happened a bit when I was younger. Voices in my head usually from like my...trainer's, I guess. Mild schizophrenia or something. I'm not sure. They don't exactly care for proper mental diagnoses in my line of work."

Conrad looked to be mulling over something. "I'm guessing you didn't really have parents who owned a small toy store in Kirillov?"

I found myself cringing at those words. The lies came back to me every night even in the arms of two alphas and resting beside Hans. I could hear the hurt present in his voice.

"No. I was an orphan. I did grow up in Kirillov but under a man who trained me to join his company of agents."

"So, like, are you a hitman? Russian Mafia?"

Despite myself, I let out a small chuckle and shook my head. "No. More like a bodyguard or a private eye. Usually for the obscenely rich like the Edwards. Vanessa hired me to root out Seraz when he started harassing their businesses."

Another pause for rumination before he spoke up again. Even though the dullness in his voice hurt, I was grateful that the conversation was being had.

"So...were you and Ross together before...?"

I grimaced. I knew exactly what he was asking. More so than just the question itself were the implications behind it. What exactly was my relationship to the alpha before all this?

"I don't know what it was. Vanessa hired me as a PI and Ross's bodyguard. This was right after Hans ran off. Back then, it was assumed he was a bored omega looking for another alpha. Now we know it was because he was running away from his father's detection. Nevertheless, Ross was heartbroken. I know he seems the most emotionally stable out of all of us but he was devastated. He loved Hans. Still does."

"Obviously," Conrad snorted. There was no jealousy or resentment but a surprising hint of fondness. I let out a small smile.

"Ross took it out on me. By that I mean he tried to woo me. Insisted on a fling. We've known each other for these past two years and I grew fond of him but I never agreed to his proposal."

I sucked in a breath as I prepared myself for the rest. I was his to judge, a sinner looking for even an ounce of redemption. "I caved in that night you walked in on us. I know-I know to hell that you don't have to believe me. I know you might think it's all bullshit. And anyway, it doesn't make it better. I still cheated on you, even if that was the first time. Even if I convinced myself that we had nothing real."

Bastard. Pathetic.

"I-I know what I did was awful. I-I know-"

Pitiful piece of sniveling rot.

"I-I-I...I'm sorry. I don't know what else to say but I'm sorry. I want you to give us another chance but I know we don't deserve it. You've been generous with giving it a month, but-but, if you want to leave..."

Conrad looked at me, finally. His beautiful eyes bore into mine. His expression was tight and unreadable. Again, I expected him to take the chance to leave me in my state of psychosis and panic.

You deserve it.

He didn't walk off. He continued to stare for a while before speaking.

"If it was all a cover...a lie....why do you want me to give you a try?" He asked slowly and carefully.

I closed my eyes. It was too great a risk to keep looking at him. I'd never bared my soul to anyone and it felt fundamentally wrong. I could feel the voice of the man who claimed to be my father telling me what a pathetic excuse for a man I was. I willed it away and let out a breath.

"Because I love you. I've never had what I had with you before then. Never had someone care for me, kiss me so tenderly. I tried telling myself it was for the best when I left. It wasn't. You're great, Conrad. I love your sarcastic wit. I love you laughing with your friends over something stupid. I love who you are." I bit my lip and looked out, over into the great vastness of the park. The crows departed and the lights of lamps twinkled in the distance.

"I'm stupid and inexperienced with these kinds of things. Plain and simple. Emotion wasn't really discussed where I came from. I know it's not an excuse. But believe me, even when Ross tried to fill the void and even when Joe and Hans came along, I knew I needed to amend things with you. Tell you the truth. And apologize. I'm sorry. I'm sorry about everything. I'm sorry and I wish the best for you, whatever happens."

My little monologue ended, and I was startled out of my daze when he chuckled. It was a deep and hearty chuckle that had me entranced. It was the same laugh we shared watching a Pixar movie in the comfort of our apartment all those nights ago.

"If I had a drink for every time you said 'I'm sorry' in that grand speech of yours I'd probably die of liver failure." There was no malice. No skepticism or bitter amusement. He looked over at me. I felt a flush of warmth and stunned surprise when he scooted over and rested his head against my shoulder.

"Y'know it'll be a bit before I can even share the same bed as you all. Even longer before I can fully trust you."

I savored Conrad's warmth against mine. Taking a risk, I tentatively wrapped an arm around him and brought him tighter and closer to me. There was something so familiar and new to it. I wanted to sit there with him for hours on end, rest and talk some more.

"I know," I murmured. I kissed the top of his fiery red hair without thinking "Take all the time you need, Solnishko. We'll wait for you."

He smiled and leaned in further. A sense of peace, if a little unsure, settled over us regardless and so did that little bit of relief wound up over months. Everything seemed right with his head on my shoulder and our hands linked together while a light flurry of snow fell.

-8-

More to come! Vote, Comment, and Follow if you're enjoying this and wish to support the author!

# Epilogue: Joe

## 2 Months Later

What exactly led up to this lovely evening where my mother was screaming at me in that high-pitched nasally voice of hers, where my stone-faced father sat and stared daggers and where my dear old brother Benjamin was sharing a smirk with his wife? Two words, I suppose. Conrad Fitzroy. That delta had become the bain of my existence since our oh so fateful meeting at some dingey gas station. Contrary to what I'd told Conrad, I didn't run off to weird and quiet places to pick up omegas who knew nothing about me. Really, it was to avoid nosey journalists, stalkers, and the makeup of snakes and weasels that I called my family.

"You-you can't do this to us! What will people think? What will people say?" My mother sobbed like a great opera actress when she needed to. The water works were on full blast tonight for my father.

"He's a liability to the firm," Benjamin piped up and his wife tried not to look too enthusiastic when she nodded in agreement. "A PR nightmare. Think of it pa. Lots of our shareholders have old-fashioned sensibilities. What of Gladstone and Comp? Of Sain-Heinz-"

"What do our shareholders have to do with Joe's dating life? Hell, what does geopolitical forecasting have to do with him dating a delta?" That was Gavin. My brother a year younger than I and a million times smarter. He was born to be a lawyer and he was the only family I could stand. I had told him of the fateful news months earlier to which he took his sweet time to "ruminate" as he called it. He told me, in that matter-of-fact voice, what exactly would happen if I were to date a delta and tell others about. Namely, that the family would not be happy, some old business partners and family friends would have their feathers ruffled and mother's friends would make snide comments till they died or until the proletariat revolution took hold and guillotined them. I would also be killed. Really, the idea was a mercy.

"This isn't about the shareholders!" Mother went on, crying like a great ingenue of the theater. Her puffy omega eyes glared holes into father, willing the old alpha to look at her and do something about this madness!

I sighed and drank my wine. Benjamin would not shut about a potential hit to the business with a smirk that would have one thinking this was good for the business and Gavin tried and failed to use his rational lawyer ways to show that all this worry was preposterous.

"We live in a new age. This will make us look progressive, liberal! We'll appeal to the millennials," Gavin continued.

"As if some bratty kids could give a shit about geopolitics. Our market base is the older-fashioned alpha looking for good sensibilities in the people that provide him information. Isn't that right father?" Benjamin went on. To his credit, my father stayed as stone-faced as ever. It was known legend that the great patriarch only ever spoke when the moons of Jupiter were aligned in a very precise and obtuse manner, reminiscent of mystic, non-euclidean geometry.

"Robert! Do something! Knock some sense into your son!" My dear mother sobbed.

That's how it went on for the rest of the evening. In the end, Gavin gave me a tight smile and shrugged. I could hear mother calling a friend to see if a trip to Hawaii was feasible in the next day or so from where I stood in the foyer, preparing to depart. Benjamin only gave me a wink and drove off in a limo where I could hear his son Quinton bawling.

The only change tonight was my father catching me before I left.

"I would have kicked you out if you hadn't brought the Edwards in as business partners. Don't fuck it up. It's the only useful thing you've done."

I gave a tight nod and left.

The original plan was to bring Conrad along to meet the family. Then I was reminded what a bad idea that was by the ever prescient Gavin. Then it was decided that Gavin would record me breaking the news to the family. The only hole in that plan was that I felt like daggers were being raked over my body at the thought of Conrad watching a recording where my family acted as if deltas were essentially the plague. He'd suffered enough.

That didn't change the promise nor the fact that Conrad was sitting in my car, a little outside the way of my parent's mansion, waiting for me to get back. What a fucking night.

I pulled on a smirk, the best that I could muster to hide the exhaustion and the irritation I felt as I strolled up to the Rolls Royce. He was playing some Cube Escape game on his phone but looked up and gave me a smile. It might have been a little strained. He was trying. That's all that mattered.

"How'd it go?"

I handed him my phone. I hadn't realized Gavin recorded my last interaction with father. I winced as his voice came up. When the video stopped, a weird silence followed. I huffed and laid back in the driver's seat.

"So that's why I don't want you to deal with them yet. They're kind of...a lot. Not Gavin. But I'd rather wait for a better time for you to meet Gavin."

Conrad nodded and bit his lip as he continued to stare down at my phone. I imagined myself kissing him, taking him like I had so many times before, biting into that bottom lip, making it bleed just a little and comforting him as he whimpered and begged for more. I imagined the lean muscles under his ratty leather jacket, running my hands over his chest and thighs and face. The tickle of his light beard, the masculine scent, the way he used to smirk against my lips. Fuck.

There was something rugged yet boyish about Conrad's body. Maybe it was the tiny bit of dominance in him, the way he teased in bed and the way he wouldn't easily submit or become pliant in my arms. Maybe it was the soft jabs, the back and forth of snark and wit. It wasn't just in bed. Our long hikes in the forests of Oregon and the mountains of Washington were filled with conversation that could last for hours on end. Sometimes, I'd step back and look at him and watch the way the light hit him in just the perfect way. The way his fiery red hair shone. The easy-going and boyish half-smile he'd shoot me. I didn't believe in soul mates. He seemed to challenge that thesis.

"Jesus. I didn't know they were so fucking awful. No offense, but your mom is kind of a psychopath."

I smiled wryly. "You should have been there for Christmas dinner when my mom found out an aunt voted differently than she did."

I contemplated switching gears and taking us back home when Conrad spoke up again.

"No, I mean it. I just...my parents were so amazingly loving. I couldn't imagine having to deal with that. Were they always like this?"

"I mean, far as I can recall. Back when I could barely piss without a diaper on and my father was already screaming at me to get into business school," I joked. Conrad had a wide-eyed look and it was amusing to find concern and sympathy in his beautiful green eyes. How to tell him not to feel too bad for the big rich alpha? I was finally with him after all, wasn't I?

He handed me the phone and laid back in his seat. "Christ. No wonder you're so emotionally constipated."

"Hey! Don't make me spank you."

A pair of sunglasses was thrown my way. "Don't make me vomit."

It went on like for a bit and it felt like heaven. My father's words dissipated for that one moment of the night and for the time that we drove back home, trading banter and mostly light jabs. It was past midnight by the time we arrived at the mansion. At the living room, there was an awkward pause. Conrad had yet to sleep with us although affections weren't completely out of the question anymore. He seemed the most comfortable around Hans and Misha and I'd be lying if I said it didn't hurt like hell but I suppose a little pain on my part was somewhat diserved.

Still, Conrad seemed hesitant to go back to his room. He stood there, rubbing his neck and looking around the area as if the modern abstract paintings on the walls were suddenly the most interesting things to him. I shrugged good night and restrained myself from kissing him even as my eyes glued themselves to his lips. Neither of us moved. He saw my look.

"Well..." I said after an awkward while. "I'll see you tomorrow-"

A kiss. God-damned, the little vixen kissed me. It was light and quick and skittish but there it was. I was too stunned to react. I might just have taken that moment to push him up against the wall and make the kiss much much longer but he hurriedly turned, muttered a goodnight and ran off to his room. My lips burned. I'd kissed him a million times before. Hell, I'd kissed him only a few months back when he'd probably almost sworn us off. It was different this time. He'd kissed me.

I felt light-headed and ecstatic as I walked up the stairs, taking a moment in the bathroom to clean up and undress. When I entered the master bedroom, my heart calmed a little at seeing Hans curled up against Misha. The omega's head was buried into Misha's chest. Soft, sandy blond hair poked out between Misha's arms encasing Hans in a firm hold. I glanced around for Ross. He was in business mode, looking down at some papers on his great oak desk on the far left side of the room. He had his own office another level up but preferred to be with us even when he couldn't sleep right away.

I stalked over and smirked, seeing him in loosened slacks and a simple dress shirt with the top few buttons undone. His sleeves were drawn to his elbows and I could see pure muscle rippling underneath. Most alphas would be ashamed to be drawn to the strength of another alpha. Benjamin still made snide remarks about our relationship. It hardly mattered to me. I'd loved Ross since I was a young boy and we'd been rooming at the Academy. He'd comfort me whenever my father had verbally or physically bashed me on any given day. He'd been there when I'd forced myself, rather stupidly, to let Conrad go.

He perked up as I sat on his desk and smiled over at him.

"I take it everything went ok?" There was a hint of exhaustion in his voice. I ran my hand through his raven black hair as I spoke.

"Yeah. Well, actually, no, my family was still shit. But that was a given. Conrad took it well though. He kissed me. I mean, yeah, it was like a second long but still. Bet you're jealous, huh?"

Ross growled playfully and leaned his head into my hand. We sat there for a minute or two in blissful peace before my father's words came back to me in a painful and cold cascade. I sighed.

"I'm definitely out of the business, though."

"I'm sure Gavin will get them to come around. Your brother is a genius." He pulled me with him as he hauled himself up and to bed. I could only give a weak and tired smile, deciding against voicing my doubts.

I all but forgot the terrible dinner with them as Ross pulled me onto the bed and into his arms. Misha and Hans shifted a bit. I listened to their soft snores and fell asleep to a small happiness I had thought died in Oregon.

# Epilogue: Ross

## 4 Months Later

"I am not taking $500!"

"Suck it up, sweetheart, it's what you're getting."

"What the hell do I need $500 for? Hans and I are checking out some souvenir shops. We need like fifty bucks asshole."

"Minimum of $500 is my final offer. Take it or leave it, Con."

"I'll leave it, dickwad."

I could feel the corner of my mouth quirk up. Lowering my sunglasses, I peaked over at the spunky little delta as he glared up at Joe. 'Little' was a bit of a misnomer. Conrad Fitzroy was a beautifully handsome man in his own right. Still, he was a feisty little kitten compared to Joe and I. Even Misha had a bit more of a lean, athletic grace. Speaking of whom.

"Should we intervene?" Misha asked as he looked up from where his head was resting on my chest. He seemed concerned and not a little unperturbed. I didn't blame him. One would think a day at the private area of the beach was just what the doctor ordered for a squabbling pair such as those two. Some peace, quiet and the rhythmic waves of the ocean in the distance. Of course, we should have all known such an idea was but a fantasy. I personally didn't mind. Joe's antics and the intriguing delta were nothing short of an endless source of entertainment. I was content to watch them from where Misha and I lay on the comfortable towel on our section of the beach.

Nonetheless, I forced myself up do to Misha's urging. Worry-filled pine green eyes seemed to be a weakness for me.

"Mind if I take sparky off your hands?" I asked. My arm wrapped up around Conrad's bare waist as I slid up behind them. The delta jumped and shot me a glare that was less intense than actual hatred. I smiled back, knowing I was giving him my best shit-eating grin. What could I say? His skin was nice and smooth and a lovely velvet against the palm of my hand. My grip tightened.

Joe huffed. "Yeah, if you teach him some manners in the process, praise be."

"Shut up," the red-head nearly growled. It was the growl of a cat against a tiger but Joe and I humored him. I mean, the kid had a back-bone! And dignity. Accepting even a little money from us was too egriguous for him but we'd slipped a few bucks here and there if he needed it or if we had a good enough excuse. I'd managed to convince Conrad to take a small (but what seemed to him an ungodly) allowance monthly. Joe, unlike I, however, was not the best salesman and his pitches only managed to irritate the fiercely independent delta.

I smiled and began dragging him to the pier.

"Hey, what about Hans?"

"Joe's going to teach him to surf," I said. I eyed the souvenir shop Conrad had been looking at since we'd come. I'd convince the delta to treat himself.

As we entered the shop, Lilian Gallahan, a dear childhood friend and fellow business associate passed by. The week-long trip to LA and it's beautiful sunset beaches was also a grueling business trip. I could only stand it with her.

"Conrad! There you are! Say, you never introduced me to that Elise friend of yours you were talking about..."

I left them to talk for a bit as I scoured the shop. My eyes landed on a beautiful carving knife only a few feet away.

"Yeah, shit, I'll give you her phone number..."

I considered the different snow globes of LA and a few fancy shot glasses. Conrad had mentioned off-hand to Hans that he had been planning on bringing back souvenirs to his friends in Tulach. How to tell him I could have paid for their stays in California as well? Smiling to myself, I considered the idea. Yes, this summer would be the perfect time. After all, I had to apologize for threatening to close down his friend's pub. The point was moot. Ross Edwards, however, hardly left his integrity to the wind. Especially not for sexy young men like Conrad. On that note, I looked over to the two again.

Lilian was by all accounts a stunning woman, probably. I couldn't really tell but men liked her enough for her good looks and her omega charm. That was beside the point. Hans was the only omega to ever catch my eye and my heart. No, the only one here that had to take my breath away was Conrad. He was lean muscle and stood in his swimming shorts and flip flops with a casual stance and a boyish smile. His hair was damp and beautifully red. How would it be to run my hand through it as I took him on the satin silk sheets of my hotel room bed?

"Well, hey, see ya tomorrow!" Lilian chimed up. She waved to me as well and set off.

By the time we'd picked out souvenirs and presents, the sun was starting to hit the horizon. Glancing at my watch, an idea popped into my head.

"We're eating seafood for dinner at the one restaurant overlooking the cruise ships," I said as we left the shop. Conrad frowned.

"I thought Hans wanted to try the Mexican restaurant."

I smiled as we headed the other way. "It'll be just you and me. Watching the sunset like in those cheesy rom-coms Hans collects."

Conrad snorted. "You sure it's not Joe? Saw him watching Pretty Woman the other day. Pretended he was doing it for Hans but I highly doubt that."

It didn't take long to arrive and it didn't take long to be seated. When I ordered the most expensive items, his eyes bulged and he began to protest but I quickly interrupted.

"Joe's told me your the Marx kind of guy. I'm merely spreading the wealth like a good comrade."

Conrad leaned back in is chair, crossed his arms and gave me a level glare. "Charity won't save you from the guillotine you capitalist pig."

It took a minute but we both laughed.

"Oh god, this is so weird."

"What's weird?" I asked as the waiter set down our drinks.

"You. Me. This. All of it. I never thought I'd be with, well, y'know. Fuck, some people are looking at us. They probably know who you are. You sure you wanna be seen with me-"

"Yes, I'm sure, Fitzroy." Without a single hesitant thought, I reached across the table, grabbed his hand and kissed it. Red fanned his face and he tried to pull back to no avail. I liked the feeling of his palm against mine and kept his hand firmly in mine as the waiter dropped off our orders. I mouthed "mine now" and he seemed hardly amused.

"You need more self-esteem," I said.

"And whose fault is that?" He shot back. Fair enough, I thought, but he'd have to eat his food with one hand. I was a stubborn bastard who'd dealt with stubborn peers, step-dads, clients and business partners all his life. What was another? And this one was a sexy red-head!

After a minute of deliberating, however, I leaned back in my seat and regarded him for a moment. Then I spoke up.

"We've put you through hell and back. So, to help with what I can, I'll let you question me now till the sun has set. Anything. Whatever you need clearing up, the heavy stuff, negotiations or, hell, we could talk about why the sky is blue."

I watched his movements like a hawk, ready to catch the smallest hair out of place. He regarded me for a moment, thinking the offer over before looking to the large window overlooking the beach and the sun. First sign that he was nervous. The kid couldn't hold my gaze.

I refrained from comforting him. My attempts might just drive him off. After the minutes passed, and I took a bite of my lobster, he began to whisper out a tentative question.

"Uum..er, how long have you and Joe been dating. How'd it happen?"

I regarded the question. There was a strangely vulnerable tone to that that I'm sure he thought I couldn't detect.

"A little after he moved to New York a few years ago. It had been after some bad break-up in Oregon. We knew each other since we were kids. Something definitely hit right when he came to New York. I spent the days comforting him and it just evolved from there." I smiled fondly at the memories. My colleagues pointed out that I had "unusual tastes" that being that I hardly cared for omegas but didn't mind taking a beta and an alpha into my arms. I could hardly muster the energy to care.

"God, Misha hated him at first. The two annoyed each other. Misha thought he was immature and Joe thought the beta was too uptight. Can't really tell you how it all worked out but it did."

I couldn't help but smile fondly. Conrad himself was supporting a sad smile. I reached across the table once again and took his calloused hand in mine where I savored the warmth and texture. The delta seemed to be ruminating on something. He looked over to me.

"He ever tell you about the 'bad break-up' in Oregon?"

I leaned forward and offered him a plate of caviar. He took it with that wary hesitance I swore I'd break away.

"Yes," I nodded. "It was only after...the shit Misha and I pulled. Joe wasn't too interested in any of Misha's missions but Misha couldn't seem to forget you. He told us about you after he ended it and then when Joe realized who you were, he also told us about your history. He was furious when he found out what Misha had done. Not that Misha was celebrating or anything."

Conrad seemed surprised. "Furious? God, I thought he hated me."

I sighed. I struggled not to pull the delta into my arms whenever he got to this way of thinking. Alphas weren't just aggressive brutes. We had a fiercely protective side. And while Conrad was nowhere near a defenseless boy, I knew he was hurting still.

"Well, as you put it, he's emotionally constipated. And terrified of his family. He's working to fix it though and I hope you know how much the moron loves you."

Conrad nodded. A nice blush overtook his handsome face. God, what I wouldn't do for a kiss.

"Alright, next question. Why were you such a jerk to Hans when we met?"

I raised a brow and frowned. "Because I also happen to be a troglodyte with mommy issues. Anyways, I thought Hans had runway, maybe even cheated like every other past lover I'd had. When he came back and explained the situation with Seraz, I practically begged Misha to punch me for being, well, in a word, a dick."

He chuckled and I followed. The sun was halfway down and we both glanced at the window in between words and bites of lobster and caviar. There was a moment where a peaceful and comforting silence took hold, where neither of us spoke and simply stared out into one part of the beauty of California. I could still feel his hand in mine and began to gently rub his palm with my thumb. He sucked in a breath. The food was mostly done.

"Want to head out and watch the sunset?" I asked in a low voice. He nodded.

The wind blew a wonderfully cool air through our hair and the sun seemed to highlight the deep orange hues in his hair. As wonderfully cliche and sickeningly romantic as it was, I suggested a walk along the mostly empty pier. Stores were closing and the beach was almost disconcertingly bare. Finally, we reached a spot where Conrad could sit on the edge of the pier and lean against the rope "fence" as he looked out into the ocean. I leaned beside him but standing on the sand below. Another moment of serene silence followed.

"I'm scared of doing it all again." The admission was a whisper and the words were choked up and strained. He sounded on the brink of tears. Without thinking, I walked between his legs and cupped the side of his face, my fingers holding his chin up and my thumb pressing against the smooth skin of his cheek.

"It's alright," I whispered. "We'll do whatever it takes to make it up to you. And if you think you're better off going your own way..." This time, my smile was just as strained and I couldn't hide the doubt plaguing my mind. Conrad shook his head. I expected him to say something more but then he asked for a kiss, blushing all the while. I didn't wait a second.

Our lips met a bit tentatively at first. I didn't want to scare him off. My hands explored his smooth back, taking in his scent, the feel of his lean and vulnerable body pressed up against mine. I shook my head, knowing it couldn't go too far. Not yet. He pulled away at about the same time. I was a bit too pleased to find his lips slightly swollen and beautifully red.

"What's wrong?" He stuttered.

I smiled and leaned my forehead against his, letting our breathes mingle. "Nothing. I just want to get to know you better. Make sure you're comfortable."

He laughed. "I guess four months still feels kind of..."

"Short?" I finished helpfully. He nodded.

I sighed and leaned back to look at him more. "Probably doesn't help that I'm busy with work. And then there's the media. If anyone ever gives you a hard time-"

"It's alright," he said. There was a bit of hesitation in him before he spoke up again. "Alright, one last question. You don't love me yet, right? Like, c'mon."

I chuckled. "You intrigue me. And it would be problematic if I weren't even a little interested, wouldn't it? Considering Misha, Joe and Hans would gut me if I hurt you." After a bit more thought, I added on, "Love you? Maybe not right now. But I'd like to get to love you and know you. I definitely like you, foul-mouthed and short-tempered as you are."

"I take offense to that," he said dryly but with a bit of humor. I couldn't but snicker and my hands found their way around his bare waist

We shared one last kiss as the sun disappeared and the stars twinkled brighter in the sky.

# Epilogue: Hans

## 1 Year Later

Conrad woke with a start. Covered in sweat, wide-eyed and panting like he'd run the Boston marathon. Misha and I stared, waiting for his breathing to level out. A small silence followed as Conrad stared at a painting on the far side of the room. Then he looked to us with a weak smile.

"Sorry. Nightmares."

"Do you want to talk-"

"Nope." Conrad was already down, his head buried underneath the pillows and blankets. Misha sighed. He followed and laid down behind the delta, hugging him from behind and slowly rubbing away the tension in the redhead's shoulders. I sat up for a bit longer, my mind wandering. Misha glanced up at me after a while. Conrad was asleep.

"You ok?"

I shook my head and slumped. "It's my fault."

"No. It's not."

It was. Even as Misha sat up and wrapped me in his arms, even as I lay my head on his shoulder and traced circles on his bare chest, I couldn't help but think about the swirling void of disaster that I seemed to inevitably bring wherever I went. If I closed my eyes, I could see my father's face, red, angry, and with a vicious back-handed slap not far behind. The image sent chills up my spine. Sometimes, I could see my father's face peeking out from our closet, outside the window or around the corner of a long corridor. He wasn't there. But he could be. He'd find me eventually.

It hardly mattered that Dominic was gone for now. The man had connections. I knew what it truly was to be tangled and caught up in the web of the underground, to be in the clutches of powerful alphas, uncaring, cruel and indifferent. I'd shown up on Conrad's doorstep and brought a glimpse of the pain with me. I'd led him into writhing tentacles waiting beneath the dark abyss.

Misha kissed my forehead. "You're thinking too much. Again."

There was a soft silence as I glanced out the window, my eyes caught in the light of the lonely moon.

"Should I tell Ross? About the hallucinations?"

Misha back-tracked when he felt me tense in his arms. I must have been shaking, looking ready to cry.

"No, no, please don't." I bit my lip to stop the trembling.

"He'll want to help you," Misha tried again. "You know he cares, Hans. He could get you a therapist. The best therapist. You and Conrad could try counseling-"

"Misha, please. I don't want to be more of a burden than I already-"

"You're not a burden."

We both jumped at the voice, low and gruff, although it was distinctly not Ross. Joe stood in the open doorway of the bedroom, cast in the yellow light trickling from the hall. He looked tired and beaten. Anyone would, dealing with his family. His white dress shirt was wrinkled, his tie undone and the slacks he'd thrown on looked ready to fall off at any moment.

As he threw his tie on Ross's leather chair, he asked, "What are you two talking about? Its two in the goddamned morning."

I looked up to Misha, urging him not to tell. Begging and pleading the best I could before the beta relented and sighed. "Conrad had a nightmare. We were about to go back sleep."

Joe grunted, struggling out of dress shirt. I couldn't help but cast a glance at the way the moonlight hit his bare chest in just the right way. He was a wall of lean, toned muscles. He caught my stare before I could even pretend to look away and held them in a threatening sort of way, letting me know that looking away was no longer an option. He was suddenly on the bed, pulling me from Misha as he shot Conrad's sleeping form a tender look.

"I know you're hiding something, little omega." My heart rate shot to a million miles a second as he took my chin between his thumb and pointer finger. Our lips brushed and the kiss lingered for a few seconds. He pulled back. "And we'll find out sooner or later. So why don't you tell us?"

"Joe," Misha sighed. I was thankful to be pulled back by the beta and tucked my head into the crook of his neck. It didn't help that the two started arguing.

"He needs to tell us. For fucks sake, Ross and I are his alphas. We'll take care of him!"

"You're not entitled to his thoughts, Joe. I know Conrad can deal with your overbearing shit but give Hans a break."

"Overbearing? Is that what it is? I just want to take care of the people I love. I just get done with another meeting with my 'family' and now I come home to be told that I'm an overbearing asshole for wanting Hans to be honest?"

"You're putting words into my mouth-"

"Am I know? I seemed to recall that-"

"Would you both kindly shut the fuck up, please and thank you?"

We all turned to find Conrad very awake and very much irritated. I peeked up at him, over Misha's shoulder. He flashed me a smile before turning to the others and scowling.

"What the hell is this all about? You're scaring Hans, and I need my beauty sleep so someone speak the fuck up."

"Language," Joe growled.

"Really, Joe? You're really going to police my speech now of all times? Well, let me fucking tell you something-"

"Conrad," Misha urged, putting a hand on the delta's shoulder that Conrad easily shook off. They were at it again. Now it was three voices, all speaking over each other, their volumes rising until the argument reached a crescendo I could no longer bear. In the cacophony of voices, I pushed myself away from Misha and sat up to face Joe and Conrad as well.

"This is my fault!"

There was a pause as they all looked to me. I wrapped my arms around myself. It was now or never. They shouldn't have to be with me because of the mess I'd wrought on.

"It's all my fault. Conrad getting roped into this and getting kidnapped. I'm the reason he has those nightmares. I'm the reason for all this," I waved my hands, indicating them, this whole mess. "I have hallucinations. Of my father. Of weird, grotesque things. He's going to come for me. I know he is. I know it's why you're all stressed. This whole thing..."

Light tears glinting in the moonlight streamed down my face. I hadn't looked up at them once since beginning my mangled mess of a monologue. "I should leave and let him have me, so-so n-no else keeps getting hur-hurt-"

I yelped as I felt myself being dragged and pulled, only to find myself in Conrad's arms. He was holding me tight and firmly to his lap. I put a hand on his chest to steady myself. Joe sat on the bed beside us, looking worn and even worse for wear. His hand wrapped around my bare foot, warming it as he looked at me quietly and with intense blue eyes. Misha scooted over. I was cocooned between the three of them.

Conrad kissed my forehead before huffing. "I guess I should have opened up about the shit going on inside my head. If only I knew... god, you really think that Hans? You've been nothing but a godsend. It's not your fault your so-called father is a piece of shit. Its his fault he's a piece of shit and we'll deal with him, ok?"

"I'm sorry." This time, it came from Joe. My heart clenched at the defeated expression on his face. "I know for a fact that I can be an asshole. I know I shouldn't feel entitled just because I'm an alpha and you're an omega. I...I don't know how else to help. I was taught to deal with omegas a certain way. Throw money at them after you let them cry over whatever issue it is they're dealing with. I want to be better. I want you to open up to us, Hans. That stuff about the hallucinations....I want to help."

Joe then made it a point to turn to Conrad and narrowed his eyes a bit. "And that means you too, sweetheart. Don't think you're getting out of this just because you're too prideful to talk about your feelings."

Conrad rolled his eyes but didn't fight Joe on that point. We were all surprised when he even reluctantly agreed. "Whatever, Darling. I-yeah, whatever, ok. Yeah."

"Amazing. I never did foresee the day when you'd all act like grown adults. I was expecting armageddon first," Misha piped up.

I bit my lip, this time to hold back a smile as Joe and Conrad ripped on Misha for thinking he was the only adult. Everything felt a little easier, much less serious and the moment was a relief. We all jumped when the door opened once again. This time, Ross stood in the doorway. He tossed aside his tie and suit jacket while giving us all a raised eyebrow.

"So, whose idea was it to have first time group sex without me? "

"Leave it to the alpha to make everything about sex. We were having a moment," Conrad huffed. Ross strode over, easy slipping off his button-up and slacks. He frowned when he saw me even as I tried to duck my head.

"Hans...have you been crying?"

I quickly rubbed away the stain of tears but he joined us on the bed, cupping my cheek and bringing my lips to his. I'm sure my face was red hot and scorching. Ross let out a low rumble.

"You were." He spoke slowly and shot a look to Conrad the delta made a point to avoid. "And you're still having your nightmares."

"I'd just promised I'd talk more about it, ok? I'm-I'm not ready for therapy or counseling or whatever. Let me process everything."

"But you'll open up to us?" Ross looked between the both of us as a hopeful lilt touched his voice. Conrad gave a hesitant nod. I smiled and couldn't help but give Ross a quick peck when an enthusiastic smile split his face. The alpha blinked and then his eyes narrowed as his smile morphed into a smirk.

I yelped as he stole me from Conrad and rolled onto the bed. I was underneath him, blushing furiously, my hands to his chest.

"Ro-Ross-"

He kissed me. A gasp escaped me and he took the moment to slip his tongue in. I could have pushed him back. My arms felt weak and already I could feel his hands, rough and possessive, riding up my hips. His kiss was punishing, rough, needy, and I let him have his way. My whimpers were met with growls and my trembling moans rewarded with his arms wrapping themselves around my smaller form and bringing me closer to him.

Our lips parted and he smiled. "I love it when you say my name. Just like that."

I caught my breath but suddenly, Joe was at my side. He stole a kiss and then Misha chuckled and took one after Joe. I was left breathless and even more so when Joe pulled Misha to him.

"You know, you've been just as much of a headache. I think a little reward for me is in order?" Joe smiled, leaning in and holding a struggling Misha close. The beta huffed and made a point to roll his eyes. It was alright. It was their usual banter.

We all stopped as a cough came from the left end of the large bed. Conrad looked awkward and out of place, slightly leaning on the headboard and pulling the blanket up to himself.

"Er, well, I'll, uh, leave you to it then...ssoo..."

Ross sighed and pulled the redhead into his arms. Conrad glanced away, biting his lip.

"Do you think you're ready?" His voice was soft and patient for an alpha as big as and as occasionally arrogant as Ross.

"I........no. I'm sorry. It's been a year and you guys have been doing great, fantastic really but even then I just-"

"You don't have to justify yourself. Take as long as you need. We'll wait for you."

That was that. Conrad looked at us, some parts apologetic, some parts surprised. His voice came out hesitant and a bit more vulnerable. It broke my heart as it did the others. We all gathered around him.

"We love you. And we'll continue to love you." I said. "It's the same as you said for me."

We shared a smile before Joe grumbled. "At least give me a kiss."

Conrad scoffed. "You and Misha wake me up at two in the goddamned morning with your old-married couple fight and expect a kiss? Make me, asshole."

Conrad almost had a look of triumph but that quickly disappeared as he realized his poor choice of words. Not a second later, Joe pounced on him. They struggled a bit but Joe seemed to have already won after stealing a few quick kisses. Conrad cursed and began throwing pillows that the alpha. Misha sighed.

As tired as I was, I couldn't help but feel an air on contentment surround me as I watched them. I leaned into Ross as we observed their antics.

As painful as the journey had been, the figurative light at the end of the tunnel seemed completely and utterly worth it. I looked about and knew that I was here with the men that I loved the most.

The End

Milton Keynes UK
Ingram Content Group UK Ltd.
UKHW030741121124
451094UK00013B/1063